D0323725

November 22, 1963

The Assassination of

President Kennedy

Brian Williams

A⁺

Smart Apple Media

First published by Cherrytree Press
(a member of the Evans Publishing Group)
327 High Street, Slough
Berkshire SL1 1TX, United Kingdom
Copyright © 2002 Evans Brothers Limited
This edition published under license from
Evans Brothers Limited. All rights reserved.

Designed by Neil Sayer, Edited by Louise John

Published in the United States by
Smart Apple Media
1980 Lookout Drive
North Mankato, MN 56003

Library of Congress Cataloging-in-Publication Data

Williams, Brian, 1943- The assassination of President Kennedy / by Brian Williams.
p. cm. — (Dates with history) Summary: Describes the events surrounding the
assassination of President John Kennedy, including the manhunt, the investigation, and
the impact on the American people and American society.
ISBN 1-58340-214-4
1. Kennedy, John F. (John Fitzgerald), 1917-1963—Assassination—Juvenile literature.
[1. Kennedy, John F. (John Fitzgerald), 1917-1963—Assassination.] I. Title. II. Series.

E842.9 .W469 2002   973.922'092—dc21   [B]   2002021026

9 8 7 6 5 4 3 2 1

Picture credits:
Corbis: 15, 16, 17, 20, 22, 23, 24, 25, 27
Hulton Getty: 6, 10, 11, 13, 21
PA Photos: 26
Topham Picturepoint: Front cover, 8, 9, 12, 14, 18

Contents

The Day the President Died

Success seemed to come easily to "JFK," and the nation had great hopes for its president.

John Fitzgerald Kennedy was the 35th president of the United States. When he became president in January 1961, he was 43 and the youngest person ever to lead the nation.

However, Kennedy was president for only 2 years and 10 months. On November 22, 1963, he was shot dead while visiting the city of Dallas, Texas. His murder shocked people all over the world.

The shooting of John F. Kennedy was a very public murder. Kennedy's last drive through Dallas was watched by crowds of people, and TV, radio, and newspapers covered every minute. The fatal seconds of the shooting were screened on TV, and replayed over and over again so that everyone who saw them never forgot them. Experts argued over what the sounds and pictures might tell about how many shots were fired, and from where.

To make matters worse, Kennedy's murderer never stood trial. A **suspect** named Lee Harvey Oswald was arrested, but was then gunned down while in police custody. No one else ever came to court. The events of that day in 1963 were examined in detail, yet for many people, mystery still surrounded the president's death.

Americans, and people in many other countries who were alive in 1963, still remember "the day President Kennedy died," and to this day, arguments about his death continue. Why was he shot? Who was to blame?

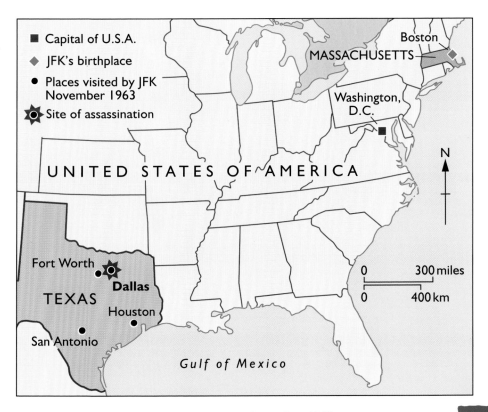

A map showing the places JFK visited in November 1963.

Kennedy for President

John F. Kennedy was not the first U.S. president to be murdered. Three presidents before him had died after being shot by an **assassin**. They were Abraham Lincoln in 1865, James Garfield in 1881, and William McKinley in 1901. Kennedy's death seemed particularly shocking because he was still young and seemed to have so much still to do as president. There seemed to be no reason or motive for his brutal killing.

The Kennedys came from Boston, Massachusetts. John was born on May 29, 1917, the second of nine children

The Kennedy family in 1938. John, aged 21, stands at the back in the center.

born to Joseph Kennedy and his wife Rose Fitzgerald. Before the Second World War Joseph Kennedy, a millionaire, had been the U.S. **ambassador** to Great Britain. During that war, John Kennedy served in the U.S. Navy, skippering a patrol boat in the Pacific Ocean.

When the war ended in 1945, John went into politics. In 1946, he was elected to Congress, and in 1952 he was elected to the Senate. In 1953, Kennedy married Jacqueline Bouvier, the elegant daughter of a wealthy financier.

The **Democratic Party** chose John Kennedy as its candidate for president in 1960. His Republican Party opponent was Richard M. Nixon, who since 1952 had served as **vice president** to President Dwight D. Eisenhower. Nixon had experience in government. Yet when the two men debated on TV, Kennedy looked confident and relaxed, while Nixon seemed anxious and ill at ease. Kennedy won, by a narrow margin.

*On January 20, 1961, the new president took the **oath** of office in Washington, D.C.*

Why Kennedy Went to Dallas

Presidents make trips all the time, across America and abroad. The reason President Kennedy went to Dallas in November 1963 was because an election was coming up, and the president wanted to boost his support in the state of Texas.

As president, John Kennedy had faced serious challenges. In October 1962, he had to show courage and determination facing the Russians over issues in Cuba. American spy photos had shown Soviet missiles on the Communist-ruled island of Cuba, which could be fired easily at the U.S. President Kennedy put U.S. armed forces on war alert, and told the Soviets to pull their missiles out of Cuba. For one extremely tense week, the world seemed close to war. Then Soviet leader Nikita Khrushchev backed down, and the missiles were finally removed.

In his first speech as president, Kennedy told Americans: "Ask not what your country can do for you—ask what you can do for your country."

At home, civil rights marches made headlines. Protesters were campaigning to end **segregation** (racial division) in some southern states, such as Alabama. President Kennedy ordered National Guard troops to protect African-American students from racist attacks.

In August 1963, civil rights leader Martin Luther King led 200,000 people in the Freedom March in Washington, D.C.

Kennedy wanted action on **civil rights** and other issues. He promised to put an American on the moon by 1970 to beat the Soviet Union to it. He spoke of a "new frontier," with better schools, hospitals, and **welfare** for all Americans. He wanted more U.S. aid for poor countries abroad.

Nineteen sixty-three was an important year in American politics. The next presidential election was due in November 1964, and the southern states were already a big worry. That is why Kennedy headed for Texas. He wanted four more years as president to achieve his goals.

The Trip to Dallas

As in 1960, the new election campaign would be run by the president's brother, Robert Kennedy, U.S. attorney general. Help would also come from other family members, including younger brother Edward Kennedy, a newly elected **senator**.

Everyone in the Kennedy camp was confident. The president was popular with many voters. Only in the southern states, such as Texas, was there any anti-Kennedy feeling. Some of his southern critics disliked him

Lyndon Johnson (center) was a hard-working politician and a loyal vice president to Kennedy.

as a northern "Yankee" who was too rich and too liberal. Kennedy was also a **Roman Catholic**, the first Catholic to be U.S. president.

Texas was the home state of Vice President Lyndon Baines Johnson, known to all as LBJ. A Kennedy visit to Texas would win votes. It would also help patch up a rift between two local Democrats, **Governor** John Connally and Senator Ralph Yarborough. The president made plans to go in November. He would stop off in five cities over three days, and enjoy dinner at LBJ's ranch.

John F. Kennedy and his wife, Jacqueline, with their children John Jr. and Caroline.

Johnson and his wife helped plan the trip, and staff members checked every detail. The Johnsons were nervous. An unfriendly Texan reception for the Kennedys would be embarrassing.

On November 21, the Kennedys said goodbye to their children and flew south to Texas.

Welcome to Dallas

The president's party made brief stops in San Antonio and Houston, where crowds cheered and the visits went well. The night was spent in Fort Worth. Next morning, Friday, November 22, they got ready for the short journey to Dallas.

The president woke at 7:30. He put on a blue-gray suit and tie. Mrs. Kennedy chose a pink suit and hat to brighten the dull day. After breakfast in the hotel, the

Crowds gathered to greet the president and his wife on their arrival at Dallas airport on November 22, 1963.

Kennedys left for the 13-minute flight to Dallas. After they landed at Love Field airport, the line of official cars headed downtown. It was 11:55.

It was customary for the president to ride in an open-topped car, so everyone could get a good look. The Kennedys sat in the rear seats of the big blue open-topped Lincoln. In the front seat were Texas governor John Connally and his wife. Next to the driver sat a Secret Service agent.

The Kennedys sat back to enjoy the drive through Dallas. They were used to the armed guards, to Secret Service agents checking every move. Other agents guarded Vice President Johnson, who rode in the next car, with Senator Yarborough. The sun was shining. It looked like it would be a good day.

The presidential motorcade sets off with its motorcycle escorts.

The School Book Depository

The sunshine made everyone feel cheerful. People along the route waved flags and took photos, and a few cheered. The Kennedys waved back from their car, now moving slowly enough for the Secret Service agents to hop off and run alongside.

The Texas School Book Depository was a grimy warehouse where school textbooks were packed for shipment.

At 12:21 the motorcade turned onto Main Street. On the right, at the corner of Houston and Elm streets, stood a building called the Texas School Book Depository. Its windows overlooked a point on the route where the presidential cars would make a zigzag as they headed for an underpass.

Inside the Book Depository, workers had stopped packing books to peer down at the president.

At a window on the sixth floor was an employee named Lee Harvey Oswald.

President Kennedy smiles at the crowds as the motorcade makes its way through the streets of Dallas.

Everyone around the president was checking watches: 12:30. In five minutes the president would be at the Trade Mart, for lunch. As the cars moved around the Z-bend at grassy Dealey Plaza, a small boy waved to the president. The president raised his hand to wave back.

There was a sound like a car backfiring. From behind the blue Lincoln, agent Clint Hill broke into a run. Senator Yarborough yelled, *"They've shot the president."*

The President Is Hit

A rifle bullet had hit President Kennedy, passed through his neck, and struck Governor Connally, who was sitting in front of him. For several seconds, time seemed to stand still. Later, trying to recall the horrific events, bystanders could not believe what they had seen. Businessman Abraham Zapruder kept on filming with his movie camera.

Then the president was hit again, this time fatally, in the head. As he collapsed, it was as if a slow-motion film had

Secret Service agent Hill leaps onto the back of the Lincoln as it speeds to the hospital.

suddenly speeded up. Driver Bill Greer put his foot down, and the Lincoln accelerated. Agent Hill leaped onto the back of the car, clinging on with outstretched hands. In the following car, agent Rufus Youngblood flung himself on top of Lyndon Johnson, to protect him from any more shots.

Sirens wailed. Frightened pigeons fluttered skyward. Some people stood still, in shock. Others looked around fearfully. The crowd scattered as the cars raced away heading for the freeway. A police radio message had already alerted Parkland Hospital.

Mrs. Kennedy cradled the body of her shot husband as the leading cars in the motorcade disappeared into the gloom of the underpass. Unaware of the shooting, drivers in the rear of the motorcade carried on toward the Trade Mart.

It took less than six minutes to speed the four miles (6.4 km) to the hospital. President Kennedy was beyond help by the time he was rushed into the hospital's Emergency Room One. In the next room lay Governor Connally, badly wounded and unconscious. Mrs. Kennedy, her clothes blood-stained, watched as the doctors frantically tried emergency treatments. It was no use. At 1:00 P.M., the president's doctor, Rear Admiral George Burkley, confirmed what Mrs. Kennedy already knew: the president was dead.

The Reaction

The news of the shooting spread with astonishing speed. News media covering a routine presidential trip were suddenly faced with a national emergency.

Newspaper headlines inform the nation of the death of President Kennedy.

Journalists ran to telephones. From 12:34 P.M. on, radio and TV stations began giving news of the shooting. Amazingly, by 1:00 P.M. almost 70 percent of Americans had heard that President Kennedy had been shot.

From the moment of Kennedy's death, Lyndon Johnson was president. He was told at 1:13 P.M., and, deeply shocked, murmured, *"Make a note of the time."* An emergency meeting of America's military chiefs was already under way in Washington. The security services switched their attention to the new president, and at 1:26 P.M. they hurried Johnson out of the hospital to the airfield. He had to get to Washington.

Flags were lowered across the nation. Radio and TV news bulletins told America that John F. Kennedy was dead. Phones were ringing across America and across the world. The president's body was taken from the hospital to the waiting plane. At 2:39 P.M., inside *Air Force One* and in front of Judge Sarah Hughes, Lyndon Johnson was sworn in as the 36th president of the United States.

Eight minutes later, the jet plane took off for Washington, carrying the coffin of the murdered president. Already the hunt was on for his killer.

Mrs. Kennedy, still in her blood-stained suit, watches as Lyndon Johnson is sworn in as president.

The Manhunt

Less than two minutes after the shooting, Dallas police officer Marrion L. Baker ran into the Book Depository, believing he had heard shots from the building. On the second floor, he stopped Lee Harvey Oswald coming out, but was told that Oswald was an employee, so he let him go and ran upstairs.

Outside the building, Oswald walked quickly away, took a bus, then a cab and arrived home at 1:00 P.M. He went out again immediately. The police were already looking for a person of his description, based on a report by an eyewitness who said he'd seen a man with a gun at a window of the Depository.

Oswald had previously been arrested in New Orleans in 1963 for protesting against U.S. policy.

At 1:15 P.M., Oswald was stopped by police officer J. D. Tippit. Oswald pulled out a revolver and shot Tippit dead. Then he ran into a movie theater, where police arrested him.

Oswald was charged with the murders of President Kennedy and Officer Tippit. Governor Connally survived. Oswald denied both charges. Newspapers, radio, and TV stations hastily put together his life story. Once a U.S. Marine, he admired Communism, had lived in the Soviet Union, and had tried to become a Soviet citizen. An Italian rifle found in the Book Depository proved to be his, bought by mail order. The Dallas police were sure they had Kennedy's killer.

On Sunday morning, November 24, the police decided to move Oswald from the city to the county jail. Suddenly Jack Ruby, a local man, ran forward and shot him. Oswald was rushed to the hospital, where he died. He would never stand trial for shooting the president.

Police officers escort Lee Harvey Oswald as he is moved to the county jail. Moments later he was shot.

The Investigation

The terrible crime of November 22 left the nation in shock. Who would want to kill America's head of state? How could such a closely guarded leader be shot? People wanted answers from the Secret Service, the **Federal Bureau of Investigation** (FBI), and the police.

On November 25, John F. Kennedy was buried in Arlington National Cemetery. Leaders of many countries attended the ceremony, and people around the world mourned a leader whose time had been cruelly cut short.

The funeral procession makes its way to Arlington Cemetery.

The death of President Kennedy was a national tragedy for the United States. Because no one was ever tried for the murder, the events of November 22 were discussed over and over again. Was Oswald the killer? Were there other gunmen? How many shots were fired?

In 1964 a government commission headed by Chief Justice Earl Warren blamed Oswald alone. Not everyone agreed. Gun experts still argued about how many shots had been fired. A congressional committee later suggested that there had been a conspiracy. Some people suggested that the real Oswald had never returned to the U.S. in 1962, but had been replaced by a Soviet agent. In 1981 Oswald's grave was opened, and scientists examined the body to make sure. It was Oswald's.

Numerous books and films have explored the events of November 22, 1963. However, for many people, the full story has yet to be told.

Jacqueline Kennedy and the president's two children at the funeral. JFK's brothers stand on either side of Jacqueline.

The Effects

After the shooting of John Kennedy, security around presidents was tightened. Today, wherever the president goes, a huge Secret Service team goes, too.

President George W. Bush arrives at the airport in Austin, Texas, accompanied by Secret Service agents.

Jack Ruby was sentenced to death in 1964 for killing Oswald, but died in 1967 while awaiting retrial. Lyndon Johnson won the election of 1964, but his presidency was to be overshadowed by the Vietnam War.

In 1968, the year Johnson decided to leave the White House, America was stunned by the assassinations of two public figures closely associated with John Kennedy. Senator Robert Kennedy, ready to make his own bid for the presidency, was murdered in Los Angeles. Civil rights leader Martin Luther King was shot dead in Memphis.

Such shootings led to calls for tighter controls on the sale of guns. Politicians continued to be targets. President Gerald Ford had two narrow escapes in 1975. In 1981, President Ronald Reagan was shot and wounded by a gunman. Foreign leaders murdered by assassins include Egypt's Anwar Sadat in 1981 and Israel's Yitzhak Rabin in 1995.

In a free society, all leaders risk attacks by gunmen or fanatics with a bomb. To protect our politicians, the security services keep tabs on likely plots and check out even the craziest-sounding rumor. After November 22, 1963, public life was never the same again.

Jacqueline Kennedy photographed with the Indian prime minister, Indira Gandhi, in 1962. Mrs. Gandhi was assassinated by her own bodyguards in 1984.

Timeline

1917   *May 29:* John Fitzgerald Kennedy is born.

1936   After prep school in Connecticut, Kennedy enters Harvard University to study government and international relations.

1939   Kennedy travels in Europe, shortly before the Second World War begins.

1941   He joins the U.S. Navy and goes to sea when the U.S. enters the war.

1943   *August 2:* His boat is sunk in the Pacific, and he is left with a painful back injury.

1944   After his brother Joe is killed in the war, Kennedy decides to go into politics when peace returns.

1946   In his first political campaign, he wins a seat in the House of Representatives.

1952   Kennedy is elected as senator from Massachusetts.

1953   *September 12:* Kennedy marries Jacqueline Bouvier.

1956   He tries to become Democratic candidate for vice president, but fails to win enough support.

1957   He wins a Pulitzer Prize for a book called *Profiles of Courage*.

1958   Re-elected to the Senate, he begins campaigning for the White House.

1960   *November 8:* Defeats Richard Nixon to win presidential election.

1961	*January 20:* Kennedy is sworn in as 35th president of the United States.
1961	Announces formation of Peace Corps. Condemns building of Berlin Wall by Communists in East Germany. Backs failed invasion of Cuba. Sends U.S. military advisers to Vietnam.
1962	*October 28:* Soviets back down, ending Cuban missile crisis.
1963	*June 26:* Visiting Berlin, Kennedy declares, "I am a Berliner."
1963	*August 28:* Tells civil rights marchers in Washington he supports their aims.
1963	*August 30:* Telephone "hot line" set up between Washington and Moscow, so U.S. and Soviet leaders can talk and settle crises quickly. This follows nuclear test ban treaty agreed to in July 1963 by U.S., U.S.S.R., and Britain.
1963	*November 21:* Kennedy leaves Washington to visit Texas.
1963	*November 22:* Kennedy is shot and killed while riding in a car through Dallas.
1963	*November 24:* The suspect, Lee Harvey Oswald, is shot dead while in police custody.
1963	*November 25:* Kennedy is buried at Arlington National Cemetery.
1963	*November 29:* President Lyndon Johnson appoints the Warren Commission to investigate the death of John F. Kennedy.

Glossary

ambassador The official representative of one country in another country, heading an embassy.

assassin Someone who murders an important person.

civil rights Freedoms and rights that should belong to all people, such as freedom of speech, freedom of religion, the right to fair and equal treatment.

Democratic Party One of the two main political parties in the U.S., the other being the Republican Party.

Federal Bureau of Investigation National crime-fighting agency of the U.S. Department of Justice.

governor Elected chief executive of a U.S. state.

oath A solemn promise made or sworn by one person before others. All U.S. presidents take an oath to obey the Constitution.

Roman Catholic Person belonging to the Roman Catholic Church, the largest Christian group, headed by the Pope in Rome.

segregation Separating people according to race, religion, or beliefs. Some southern U.S. states had separate schools for blacks and whites before the 1960s.

senator Elected member of the Senate, which is one of the two houses of the U.S. Congress. The other house is the House of Representatives.

suspect Person questioned by the police in connection with a crime.

vice president Deputy to the U.S. president.

welfare Government programs to help people in need, such as the poor, old, sick, and unemployed.

Index

22 November 1963 22 November 1963